Hueber
Lektüren

The Show Must Go On

Sue Murray

Illustrated by Jacqui Grantford

This is the German version of **The Show Must Go On**

The Show Must Go On
Created and developed by
International Language Teaching Services Pty Ltd
4/2 Forsyth Street
Glebe NSW 2037
Australia

Author: Sue Murray
Series editor: James Bean
Illustrations: Jacqui Grantford
Text design: ILTS Pty Ltd

3. 2. 1. Die letzten Ziffern
2010 09 08 07 06 bezeichnen Zahl und Jahr des Druckes.
Alle Drucke dieser Auflage können, da unverändert, nebeneinander benutzt werden.
1. Auflage

Redaktion: Heike Birner
Umschlaggestaltung: Parzhuber & Partner, München
Umschlagfoto: © Brand X Pictures
Druck und Bindung: Ludwig Auer GmbH, Donauwörth
Printed in Germany
ISBN 3-19-292960-X

Contents

Chapter 1

Hamlet comes to school

On the way to school one day, Fraser said to Tom, 'Do you want to come and see *Hamlet* at the City Theatre on Saturday afternoon? My father is going to take me. He said you can come too.'

Tom Clark and Fraser McDonald were best friends. They loved going to the theatre to see plays. They both wanted to be actors. They went to acting lessons in the city every Monday afternoon. Fraser liked to dance too. He went to tap dancing classes every Saturday afternoon. He loved the sound his tap dancing shoes made. Tom didn't learn tap dancing. He played football for the school every Saturday.

'*Hamlet* is a play by William Shakespeare,' said Fraser.

'I know that,' said Tom. 'I want to play Hamlet one day.' He jumped in front of Fraser and said in a loud voice, 'To be or not to be, that is the question!'

'Very good, Tom. Do you want to come?'

'Yes, I'd love to see it. Thanks! Who's playing Hamlet?'

'Heath Mason!' said Fraser.

'Wow!' said Tom.

Heath Mason was an actor in a television show called *Here and Now*. He played a young doctor, Doctor Carson. The boys watched the show every Monday night.

'I really want to see *Hamlet*,' said Fraser. 'So I won't go to tap dancing class this Saturday. My dancing teacher will understand. She loves Heath Mason too!'

Tom stopped walking. 'Oh, no!'

'What?' asked Fraser.

'I can't come to the play. I have to play football on Saturday,' said Tom. 'We have an afternoon game – against Riverdale High. Mr Rankin won't understand.'

'Ask him, Tom. You have to come!' said Fraser.

'I'll ask him at training after school today,' said Tom. 'But he won't be happy.'

After football training that afternoon, Tom said to his coach, 'Can I speak to you, please, Mr Rankin?'

'What is it, Tom?' Mr Rankin, the football coach, was a short man with a red face. He always yelled at the players.

'It's about the game on Saturday,' said Tom.

'What about it?' said Mr Rankin.

'I don't want to play in it, sir,' said Tom.

'What? Why not?' yelled Mr Rankin. 'You are the best player I have.'

'Um – I want to go to the theatre. Heath Mason is in *Hamlet*.'

'The theatre? We're playing Riverdale on Saturday!' Mr Rankin was angry. 'No, Tom. We need you. Forget about going to the theatre.' Mr Rankin walked away.

Gary Howard walked over to Tom and said, 'Listen, Clark, you're not the best player. I am. But you be at that game on Saturday. Or I'll come and get you.'

Gary Howard was the biggest boy in the football team. He was strong. He had very large hands. He put a hand in front of Tom's face.

'Hello, Tom. Hello, Gary,' a voice said. It was Fraser. He stood next to Tom.

Gary put his hand down and said, 'Be there on Saturday, Clark. Or I'll find you.' He walked away.

'What was that about?' asked Fraser.

'Mr Rankin said I was the best player. Gary heard him.'

'Oh,' said Fraser. 'Gary did look angry! Can you come and see *Hamlet*?'

'No,' said Tom. 'I'm in the team. I have to play football on Saturday, Fraser.'

At lunchtime the next day, Fraser came running to Tom. 'Tom! He's here at our school! Hamlet's here!'

'*Who's* here?' asked Tom.

'Heath Mason. I saw him talking to the teachers.'

'Heath Mason – here? Where is he?'

The boys hurried through the school.

'There he is!' yelled Fraser. 'At the school hall. He's going into the school hall!'

Tom and Fraser ran into the hall. The boys looked for the actor, but they couldn't see him.

'It's empty,' said Tom. 'Did you really see him?'

'I did,' said Fraser. 'It was him.'

They went up onto the stage.

'Hey, Fraser, you be Hamlet and I'll be the king,' said Tom. 'Come, Hamlet, come, and take this hand from me!'

Just then, Heath Mason walked onto the stage. 'Hello,' he said. 'That's very good.'

The boys looked at him.

'I'm Heath,' he said.

'I know!' said Tom. 'You're Heath Mason!'

Heath Mason smiled and walked across to the boys. 'Who are you?' he asked.

'Er, I'm Tom and this is Fraser. But what are you doing here?'

'I'm an old boy of this school,' said Heath.

'You are?' said Tom.

'Yes. I was a student here. I left twelve years ago. I acted in my first play here on this stage.'

'Fraser and I love acting,' said Tom. 'But the school doesn't put on plays now.'

'That's sad,' said Heath. 'My English teacher, Miss Piper, put on the school plays then. Does she teach here now?' he asked.

'No. Fraser and I go to an acting school in the city,' said Tom. 'We put on plays there.'

'I'm coming to see you in *Hamlet* on Saturday,' said Fraser.

'Good! Are you coming too, Tom?' asked Heath.

'I want to, but I can't. I have to play football.'

'Mr Rankin was my football coach,' said Heath. 'Does he teach here now?'

'Yes,' said Tom. 'He's my coach too.'

'He loves football, doesn't he?' smiled Heath.

Just then, some teachers came into the hall. The school principal, Mr Barton, was with them. He walked up to the stage and said, 'Ah, there you are, Heath. We didn't know where you were.'

'I just wanted to come and look at the hall. I love this place. I did some plays here,' Heath told Mr Barton.

'Ah yes,' said Mr Barton. 'That was before my time here.'

Tom saw Mr Rankin at the back of the hall. Heath saw him too. 'Hello, Mr Rankin,' he called.

'Hello, Heath,' said Mr Rankin. He walked up to the stage.

'Tom can't see my play on Saturday because he has to play football,' said Heath. 'Can't he come to my play?'

'No, he can't,' said Mr Rankin. 'We need him. We're

playing Riverdale. It's the biggest game of the year. You played in the team when you were a student here, Heath. You know Tom has to play on Saturday.'

Heath looked at Tom. 'Mr Rankin's right. You should play football on Saturday, Tom. Come and see my next play.'

Mr Barton said, 'Boys, go to class. Mr Mason will be talking to the school soon.'

'Goodbye, Heath,' said Fraser.

'Thanks for asking about Saturday,' said Tom. 'Nice to meet you.'

'Goodbye, Tom. Goodbye, Fraser,' said Heath.

Outside, Fraser said, 'Wow! We met Heath Mason!'

'But why is he here?' asked Tom.

'I don't know,' said Fraser.

In the afternoon, all the classes had to go to the hall. Tom and Fraser went with their English class. This time, the hall was full of students and teachers. Mr Barton walked onto the stage.

'Today we have a visitor. He is an old boy of the school. He was a student here before any of you came here. But you all know him. Here he is – Mr Heath Mason.'

All the students started talking. Then Heath walked onto the stage and there was a lot of cheering and clapping. Some students stood up. Teachers yelled at the students to sit down and be quiet. Then Heath smiled and raised his hands and all the students sat quietly.

'Thank you, Mr Barton,' said Heath. 'Good afternoon, boys. It's nice to be back at my old school. I'm here to talk about being an actor. It's not an easy job, but I love it. I started acting here on this stage when I was fifteen. And now I want you to act on this stage too.'

Tom looked at Fraser. What was Heath going to say next?

'I've spoken to Mr Barton about this. I want some of you to try acting. So there is going to be a play competition. There will be prizes for the best play and the best actor. I will come back here five weeks from now. I'll watch the plays that you put on. The group that puts on the best play in the competition will come to the first night of my next play at the City Theatre in November. I'll be doing Shakespeare's *As You Like It*. You can come and meet the other actors in the play. And the best actor in the competition will be on my television show, *Here and Now*, for a day. One boy from this school will play my little brother!'

There was a lot of noise from the students.

'That will be me,' said Tom quietly.

'That will be me,' said Fraser quietly.

Both boys wanted that prize. But only one boy could win the competition.

Chapter 2

We can't do that!

Tom and Fraser were very excited about the competition.

'We need to find a good play to put on,' said Tom on the way home from school.

'Yes. The library was full of boys after school,' said Fraser. 'They were all looking for books of plays.'

'The library doesn't have many plays,' said Tom.

'Tom! Fraser! Wait for us!' called a boy with long black hair. It was their friend, Luke Reed. Luke was with Anton Mitchell. All four boys were good friends. Tom and Fraser waited for Luke and Anton. Then the four boys walked along the street.

'So, what play are we going to do?' asked Luke.

'We?' said Tom. 'But you don't like plays, Luke.'

'Yes, I do,' said Luke. 'Don't look so surprised. It'll be fun.'

'Luke wants to win the competition. He wants to go on television,' said Anton. 'I don't. But I do want to be in a play.'

'But Anton, you and Luke have never done any acting,' said Fraser. 'It's not easy.'

'You can teach us,' said Anton. 'What kind of play shall we do?'

'We can do any kind of play. It can be funny or sad,' said Tom. 'It must be no longer than fifteen minutes.'

'Let's do a funny play,' said Luke. 'I like to make people laugh.'

'Me too,' said Fraser. 'But maybe Heath Mason likes sad plays. He is doing *Hamlet*.'

'We should do the play that is right for us,' said Anton.

'You're right, Anton,' said Tom. 'We have to find the right play. Let's all look for one and meet at my house after school on Friday. Everyone bring one play.'

'I'll go to the bookshop,' said Fraser.

'Good,' said Tom. 'And I'll visit my grandfather. He has a lot of books. Maybe he has some books of plays.'

The group met on Friday.

'You go first, Luke,' said Tom. 'Did you find a play?'

'Yes. I brought this book,' said Luke. He showed it to the group. 'It has some very funny plays in it. I like this one the best – *Monkey Man*. It's about a man who can turn people into monkeys.'

'I don't want to be a monkey in front of the school,' said Anton.

'Oo-oo-ooh!' Luke made loud monkey noises and started jumping about. Fraser laughed and jumped about too. They made louder and louder monkey noises.

'Quiet, you two!' yelled Tom. He was looking at Luke's book. 'Luke, *Monkey Man* has ten people in it. There are only four of us.'

'And I don't want to be a monkey on stage!' said Anton.

'So what did you find, Anton?' asked Luke.

Anton showed them a book of plays by William Shakespeare. 'I really like these.'

'And Heath Mason likes Shakespeare too,' said Fraser. 'But his plays are much too long. And they have a lot more people than *Monkey Man*.'

'Monkey man! Oo-oo-ooh!' yelled Luke. He jumped up again.

'Quiet, Luke!' yelled Anton. He opened the book. 'Look.

This is *Romeo and Juliet*. We don't have to do all the play. We can just do these pages here. It's when Romeo is in a fight.'

'I'll be Romeo!' yelled Luke.

'I'll fight you!' yelled Fraser. The two boys ran around the living room.

'Stop it!' yelled Tom. Then he said, 'I like *Romeo and Juliet* too, Anton. But maybe it's too hard for us. And I want to do something new. What did you find, Fraser?'

'I've got one called *Taylor, Taylor*,' said Fraser. 'It's new. It's about a boy and a girl who have the same name.'

'I don't want to be a girl in front of the school,' said Anton.

'It's better than being a monkey,' said Fraser.

'Monkey man!' yelled Luke, and he jumped up again.

'Quiet!' said Tom. 'I went to see my grandfather. We looked at a lot of plays. But they were all too long or they had too many people in them.'

'So you don't have a play to show us?' said Anton.

'No,' said Tom.

'Okay, we'll do *Monkey Man*, then,' said Luke. 'Oo-oo-ooh!'

'No. I'm not doing that play,' said Anton. 'Let's do *Romeo and...*'

'No,' said Fraser. 'No Shakespeare.'

'And I don't want to be a girl in Fraser's play,' said Luke.

Everyone in the group started yelling.

'My play!'...'No, my play!'...'*Monkey Man!*'...'We can't do that!'

'QUIET!' yelled Tom.

'You don't even have a play,' said Luke angrily.

'No, but listen,' said Tom. 'We want to do a new play, right? So let's write a play.'

The group looked at Tom. 'Fraser and I have written short plays at our acting school,' he said.

Fraser smiled. 'My play was bad. I can dance and act but I can't write. But you write well, Tom. Your play was very good.'

'Let's do that one,' said Anton.

'We can't. It has twelve people in it. I wrote it for our acting class,' said Tom. 'But I can write a new one. I'll write a play for four people, just for us.'

'We don't have much time,' said Anton. 'The competition is only a month away.'

'You can do it, Tom,' said Fraser. 'You'll write a really good play.'

'What will it be about?' asked Anton.

'I don't know yet,' said Tom.

'I want a play with tap dancing in it,' said Fraser.

'And drums!' said Luke. 'I want to play drums!'

'Let's meet here again on Sunday,' said Tom. 'I'll tell you what the play will be about then.'

Chapter 3

Finding the story

The next day was Saturday, the day of the big game against Riverdale. Luke and Anton came to watch the game. Fraser went to see Heath Mason in *Hamlet*.

'How is the writing going, Tom? What's your idea for the play?' asked Luke before the game.

'Have you written it yet?' asked Anton.

'I haven't had time to do any writing,' said Tom. Tom didn't know what to write about yet. He had no idea. He wanted to write a really good play and win the competition. But he didn't know what to do. It was hard. He hadn't slept much. He was very tired.

Mr Rankin came across the football field. 'Tom!' he yelled. 'The Riverdale team is here already. Get out on the field and play hard. We must win this game!'

Anton and Luke watched the game. 'Come on, Tom,' they yelled. 'You can do it!'

But Tom played very badly. He was too tired.

Gary Howard ran up to him on the field. 'You're the worst player, Clark!' he said. 'A girl can kick better than you.'

Tom said nothing. Gary was right. He was playing very badly.

'Here comes the ball!' said Gary. He ran after the ball and kicked it hard. 'Yes!' he yelled and jumped in the air. Gary was playing well.

Mr Rankin yelled from the side of the field. 'Tom Clark, come off the field now!'

Mr Rankin told another boy to play. Tom walked slowly

off the field. Mr Rankin yelled at him, 'What's wrong with you? Are you ill?'

'No, sir,' said Tom.

Tom's team won the game. But Mr Rankin wasn't happy. 'We have three more games this year. We must win them all,' he said to them. 'Tom, you played very badly today. The team needs you to play well. Gary, you were the best player today. But every boy in this team must play better. I want to win!'

When Tom was unhappy, he often visited his grandfather.

'Hello, Granddad,' said Tom.

'Hello, Tom. What's wrong?'

Tom told his grandfather about the football game. And about what Mr Rankin said.

'We all have good days and bad days, Tom,' said his grandfather. 'You'll play better next time. Forget it. Let's talk about your play. How's it going?'

'Not very well. I can't think of a story,' said Tom.

'When I want to find a good story, I read this,' said his grandfather. 'It's full of good ideas.'

Tom's grandfather gave Tom a big old book.

'*Stories from Old Greece*,' Tom read.

'You'll find a good story in there,' said Tom's grandfather.

'Thanks, Granddad,' said Tom.

Tom took the book home and read it that night.

In the morning, he had an idea for the new play.

On Sunday, the group met at Tom's house.

'Heath Mason was a really good Hamlet,' said Fraser. 'And I loved the fight at the end of the play!' Fraser jumped up. He showed his friends some of the fight.

Stories from Old Greece

'Okay, Fraser,' said Tom. 'We have to get on with our play now. We only have a month.'

'What play are we doing, Tom?' asked Luke.

Tom smiled and said, 'I'm writing a play called *Fire Light*. It's about a man called Prometheus.'

'Proth…Who?' said Luke.

'I know the story of Prometheus,' said Anton. 'He gave fire to men, didn't he?'

'Yes,' said Tom. 'I read the story in a book last night. Prometheus made men out of clay.'

'Clay?' said Luke. 'My mum makes flower pots out of clay. She makes coffee cups out of clay too. But making men out of clay?'

'It's an old story, Luke,' said Tom. 'A Greek myth.'

'Okay. So in this myth, Prometheus made men out of clay. Is that what the play is about?'

'Wait and listen, Luke,' said Tom. 'Prometheus made men out of clay and he taught them a lot of things. He taught them to grow food and he taught them to fight.'

'To fight? Can we have fighting in the play?' asked Luke.

'Maybe,' said Tom. 'But that's not the end of the story. The men didn't have fire. Zeus, the king of the gods, didn't like men. Zeus didn't want them to have fire. But Prometheus wanted to give fire to his men. So he went to the place where the gods did their cooking. He took some fire. He stole fire from the gods. But Zeus wanted a world without fire. So Zeus was very angry with Prometheus.'

'Do they fight?' asked Luke.

'Be quiet, Luke,' said Anton. 'I really like this myth, Tom. It will make a good play.'

'We have a lot of work to do,' said Tom. 'Are you guys all happy to do this story?'

'Yes!' they all said.

'Then let's get to work. And can you all come here after school on Tuesday? We'll need to work hard on this play,' Tom said. 'We'll need to rehearse a lot.'

'We'll need to do what?' asked Luke.

'Rehearse. We'll need to do the play again and again to get it right.'

'We mustn't tell any other boys about this,' said Anton. 'We don't want another group to steal our idea.'

'Anton is right,' said Fraser. 'We mustn't talk about this to the other groups.'

'On with the show!' said Luke. 'I want to be Prometheus.'

'No, I want to be Prometheus!' said Fraser.

'It's my idea,' said Tom. 'So I'm going to be Prometheus.'

'Quiet!' yelled Anton. 'Don't fight or we won't have a show!'

'I'm going home,' said Fraser.

'Me too,' said Luke.

They left.

'Oh well, I'll go too,' said Anton. 'I like your idea, Tom. And I don't want to be Prometheus. I just want to be in the play.'

'Thanks, Anton,' said Tom.

Tom needed Fraser and Luke to do his play. Without them, there was no group and no play. That night, he phoned Fraser.

'Hi, Fraser,' Tom said. 'Listen, you can be Prometheus. You're the best actor in our group. And you can dance. I'm the writer and I want Prometheus to dance in our show. Luke can be Zeus. He'll be the king of the gods. And Zeus can play drums. Luke will like that idea. Anton and I can be the other people in the play.'

'Really? Thanks, Tom,' said Fraser. 'But then you won't win the best actor prize. You won't do much acting.'

'But I'll write the play. Maybe it will win the prize for the best play.'

'It will. I know it will,' said Fraser.

Tom phoned Luke next. Luke liked the idea of being Zeus. He loved the idea of playing the drums.

Then Tom phoned Anton. 'Hi, Anton,' he said. 'It's going to be okay. Luke and Fraser are happy now. I am too. The show can go on.'

Chapter 4

Losing a man

The group worked hard for the next two weeks. Tom wrote the play very quickly. The boys all learnt their words. They had a lot of fun.

Tom tried hard at football too. One day Mr Rankin said, 'Well done, Tom. You're playing very well.'

Gary came close to Tom and said, 'I'm better than you. You're hopeless.' Then he hit Tom on the arm.

'I saw that, Gary Howard!' yelled Mr Rankin. 'Don't hit other players. Do you understand?'

'Yes, sir,' said Gary. Then he said quietly to Tom, 'Why do you play football, Clark? You're always doing your acting. Footballers should just play football.'

'I can do both.'

'Oh yeah? Your group's play is hopeless,' said Gary.

'It's not hopeless,' said Tom. 'We're going to win.'

'All plays are hopeless,' said Gary and he walked away. Tom watched him go.

The group rehearsed often – some days in a classroom after school, some days at Tom's house. Fraser worked hard on the tap dance for Prometheus. Luke loved playing the drums when he walked onto the stage. Tom and Anton were the men of clay. Anton and his mother made the costumes for the play. Luke liked his costume – Zeus wore a big purple coat.

Anton made masks for the group. The masks went over the top half of their faces. The boys could wear their masks and say their words. The mask for Zeus was golden. The mask for Prometheus was white. The masks for the men of clay were brown.

Homework
Revise Quadratic
equations p46.
Due Tue.

'I like my golden mask,' said Luke. 'The sun is golden. So is Zeus. I'm the king of the gods!'

Then one Wednesday, Anton didn't come to school. That afternoon, the phone rang at Tom's house. Tom answered it.

'It's Mrs Mitchell here, Tom – Anton's mother.'

'Hello, Mrs Mitchell. How are you?'

'I'm fine, but Anton is sick. He's got glandular fever.'

'Oh, no!' said Tom.

'Yes. He was very tired last night and this morning he was really sick. We went to the doctor and he said it was glandular fever.'

'Will he be okay?'

'Yes, but he has to stay home from school for a few weeks. He wanted me to phone you, because he won't be able to be in your play. It's sad – he really wanted to be in it.'

'That's really bad news. I hope he gets better soon,' said Tom. 'Oh, Mrs Mitchell, the costumes and masks – Anton has them.'

'Oh yes, that's right. I'll get them to you over the weekend. Is that all right?'

'Yes. That will be fine,' said Tom. 'Thanks, Mrs Mitchell. And I'm sorry about Anton.'

Tom told Luke and Fraser the bad news the next day.

'Maybe we can find another boy to be in our play,' said Luke.

'But who?' said Fraser. 'Everyone's in a play already.'

'Maybe we'll have to make a boy out of clay!' said Luke.

'Ha, ha. Not funny,' said Fraser.

'There's no time to write the play again,' said Tom.

'I know,' said Fraser. 'The competition is at the end of next week.'

'And my last football game is only two days away,' said

Tom. 'I need to get some sleep tonight.'

At football training that afternoon, Tom tried to forget about the play. He tried to forget about Anton. He tried to kick the ball well. Gary Howard kept running in front of Tom. Tom fell over.

'Get up, Tom,' yelled Mr Rankin. 'It's not time for bed yet.'

The team laughed. Gary laughed the loudest.

'Maybe he's tired, sir,' said Gary. 'Maybe he's too tired to be in the game on Saturday. He's been doing his play all the time.'

'I don't want to hear any more about those plays. We're here to play football,' said Mr Rankin. 'Now boys, one of you will have to watch the game on Saturday. We have too many players. So one of you won't play. Think about that. Okay, back to work. I want to see fifteen more minutes of hard football before we finish today.'

The boys played again. Gary stood near Tom and the ball came towards them. Tom kicked it, but then Gary hit Tom.

'Right, that's it!' yelled Mr Rankin. 'I've told you before, Gary Howard – no hitting. You're out of the team for Saturday.'

'What?' said Gary. 'But I'm the best player, sir.'

'Not another word, boy,' said Mr Rankin. 'You're not going to play.'

'Oh, sir…' said some of the other boys.

Tom said, 'Can I play half the game, sir? Then Gary can play the other half.'

'No, Tom. Gary can sit and watch,' said Mr Rankin and he walked away.

Gary was very angry. 'I don't need your help, Clark,' he said to Tom in a nasty voice.

Anton phoned Tom on Friday evening.

'How are you?' asked Tom.

'Not good,' said Anton. 'Glandular fever is no fun. I'm really tired all the time. Listen, I'm sorry about the play.'

'That's okay, Anton.'

'And good luck in the football game tomorrow. My mum will bring the costumes and masks to you then. Okay?'

'Okay,' said Tom. 'You just get better.'

'I'll try. Maybe I'll be a little better by the end of next week. Then I'll be able to come and see the play. I'd like to see my costumes and masks on the stage. And I'd like to see you guys win the competition.'

The day of the last football game was cold and wet. Luke and Fraser came to watch the game. Most of the school came to watch. Gary Howard was there. He was not happy. He didn't want to sit on the side.

The first half of the game was hard. The other team was very good. Tom had to play his very best football. He was tired and cold and wet. It was hard to play in the rain.

'Please can I play now, Mr Rankin?' asked Gary after the first half.

'No,' said Mr Rankin. 'The team's playing well without you.'

Gary looked very sad.

'Okay, boys, I want a good, hard, fast second half. Go out there and win!' said Mr Rankin.

They did win. There was a lot of cheering. But not from Gary. He went up to Tom. 'I should have played today, Clark, not you.'

Luke and Fraser ran up to Tom and yelled, 'You won! You won! You were great!'

'Thanks, guys,' said Tom.

'Well done, Tom!' said Mrs Mitchell. She was carrying a big bag. 'Here are the costumes and masks,' she said. 'Good luck with the play, boys.'

'Thanks, Mrs Mitchell,' said Tom. 'Say hello to Anton for us.'

Luke and Fraser left, and Tom carried the bag to the changing room at the side of the field. The boys in Tom's team were all in the changing room.

Tom put the bag down and got changed. He took off his wet football clothes and he put on some warm, dry clothes.

'We won! We won!' yelled the boys in the team. There was a lot of noise – yelling and singing and laughter. Mr Rankin had a big smile on his face.

Half an hour later, most of the boys were leaving the changing room. It was time for Tom to go home too. He looked for the big bag. He looked under all the seats in the changing room. The bag was gone!

Where could it be? Suddenly, Tom knew.

He went to an old house at the far end of town. There were some old broken chairs outside the front door. A fat man with no hair was sitting there. His clothes were dirty.

'Hello…um…Mr Howard?'

'What do you want?' the man said in a nasty voice.

'Is Gary home?' asked Tom.

'Who are you?'

'I'm Tom Clark. I'm…I go to school with Gary.'

'His room's at the back,' said Mr Howard. 'Go in.'

Tom went inside. The house was dark. He walked to the back of the house and looked in a bedroom. Gary was there and the bag of costumes was at his feet. He was wearing the golden mask and the purple coat and looking at himself in a mirror. He didn't see Tom. Tom didn't say a word.

Then Gary saw him. He quickly took off the mask and coat and threw them across the room. 'What are you doing here?' he shouted. 'Get out!' His face was red.

'You took our costumes and masks,' said Tom. 'Why?'

Gary didn't reply.

'Why did you take them, Gary?'

Then Gary spoke in a quiet voice. 'You want to do everything, don't you? You play football and…and you do your plays and you…Just take your stupid things and get out!'

He turned away from Tom. Tom was angry but then he heard Gary make a noise. Was he crying?

'Gary,' said Tom. He had an idea. 'Gary, wait. Would you like to be in our play?'

'What?' said Gary. He turned and looked at Tom. His eyes were wet.

'Would you like to be in our play?' Tom said again.

'Me? In your play? Don't be stupid!'

'But we need you. Anton can't do it. He's sick. We need another actor. Please, Gary.'

'No,' said Gary. 'I don't want to.'

'Please, Gary,' Tom said again. 'It'll be fun. There's fire in it. And drums.'

Gary didn't speak for a long time. Then he said, 'Okay.'

Chapter 5

Fire Light

'What?' yelled Fraser.

'You asked Gary Howard?' said Luke.

'Why?' asked Fraser.

Tom looked at Luke and Fraser. 'Gary isn't in another play. And he really wants to be in our play. We have one week to go and we need him. Come on, guys. Let's try doing the play with Gary.'

Luke looked at Fraser. Fraser looked at Luke. 'Okay,' said Fraser.

'Here he comes now,' said Tom.

The new group rehearsed very hard. Gary really liked being a man made of clay but he often forgot his words. Three days before the competition, Gary forgot his words again. 'I'm hopeless, aren't I?' said Gary to Tom.

'No, you're not,' said Tom. 'You've worked very hard. I'm really happy you're in our play, Gary. We couldn't do it without you.'

The day before the competition, the boys went to the school hall. All the groups had to rehearse their plays in front of the teachers and the principal. Tom and his group were third.

The first group did some pages from *Macbeth*. 'It's good that we're not doing a play by Shakespeare,' said Fraser quietly.

The second group did a funny play. 'Oh, that was very good,' said Luke. 'Maybe they'll win.'

Then Tom's group went on stage. *Fire Light* went well. At

the end, Fraser came on stage. He was tap dancing and carrying a stick. The stick was on fire. He danced over to Tom and Gary. They held a big golden bowl. Fraser put the stick into the golden bowl. Then the bowl was full of fire. 'I, Prometheus, give you fire!' said Fraser.

'Stop!' Mr Barton called out. 'Stop the play!'

Fraser stopped dancing.

'What's wrong, sir?' asked Tom.

'Put that fire out now!' said Mr Barton.

Tom and Gary put out the fire.

'You cannot have fire on stage,' said Mr Barton.

'But we must have fire for our play, sir!' said Tom. 'It's all about fire.'

'Not in this hall. Get off the stage now,' said Mr Barton. 'Next group, please.'

What could they do? Was this the end of their play?

'I have an idea,' said Tom to the group. He went over to Mr Barton. They had a long talk. Luke, Fraser and Gary stood and watched them. Then Tom came back to the group.

'It's okay. The show must go on! And it will. Listen...'

It was the night of the competition. Heath Mason was in the hall. A lot of boys and their families were there. Anton was there with his mother and father. It was a big night. There were ten plays. Tom's group was the last group of the night.

The other groups did their plays. Some of the plays were very good. Then it was time for Tom's group. Tom went up on stage. He spoke to the people in the hall.

'For the last play, please follow us outside to the football field.'

There was a lot of noise. Go outside? Why? People slowly went out of the hall and onto the football field. It was a very

cold night but there were no clouds. The stars and the moon shone in the night sky.

'Now, please stand in a big circle around here,' said Tom. He pointed to a large pile of sticks on the ground. The people all moved and stood in a circle around the sticks. Then Luke played his drums and the actors walked into the circle. On with the show!

At the end of the play, Fraser lit the golden bowl of fire. Then Gary and Tom carried the golden bowl to the pile of sticks. They put the golden bowl onto the pile, and the fire from the bowl lit the sticks. The fire danced high into the night sky. Prometheus gave fire to men.

Nobody spoke. Tom and his group stood quietly. They took off their masks. Then the crowd started cheering and clapping. The boys smiled.

'They liked it,' said Fraser.

Heath Mason stepped close to the big fire and held up his hands. 'Thank you to all the groups. I really liked the plays tonight. A lot of work has gone into all of them. Now it's time to say who has won. The prize for the best play goes to *Fire Light*!'

There was a lot of clapping and cheering.

Tom said to Anton, 'Come with us. You made the masks and costumes. You were one of the group.'

The five boys went and shook hands with Heath.

Heath held up his hands again. 'And the prize for the best actor goes to Prometheus in *Fire Light* – Fraser McDonald.'

Fraser looked at Tom. 'Thanks, Tom,' he said quietly. Then Fraser walked over to Heath and shook hands with him again.

'You are a very good actor, Fraser,' said Heath. 'You'll

play my little brother very well.' Heath looked around the circle of people and said, 'One more thing. I want to ask the boy who wrote *Fire Light* to meet the writers of *Here and Now*. We need good new writers for television.'

A short time later, the group stood by the fire. A lot of people had left. It was late.

'Wow! That was the best fun!' said Luke.

'Thanks to Tom,' said Fraser. 'You wrote the best play!'

Tom smiled and smiled. He said to Gary, 'You weren't hopeless!'

Gary laughed. 'No, I wasn't. I love being an actor.'

Heath Mason walked over to them. 'I love being an actor too!' he said. 'I remember doing plays here at school, but we never did a play out here. That was a very good idea. I have to go now, but I'll see you all in November. Fraser and Tom, the people from *Here and Now* will speak to you two next week.'

'Thanks, Heath,' said Tom. 'Thanks for bringing plays back to our school.'

'Ha! Just like Prometheus bringing fire to man!' said Anton.

They all laughed.

Activities

Chapter 1

Before you read

A. Look at the picture on page 6 and circle the correct answers.

1. Where are the boys?
   a. at the theatre b. on a football field c. at the beach
2. How does the boy on the left look?
   a. friendly b. unfriendly c. sad

B. Find these words in your dictionary. Use them in the sentences.

actor cheering hall stage

1. There was a lot of __________ when the game began.
2. The singer walked onto the __________ and began to sing.
3. This __________ is big. It can hold two thousand people.
4. When I was a child I wanted to be an __________ and be on TV.

C. Listen to Track 3 on the CD and answer these questions.

1. Did Tom want to go to see *Hamlet*?
   a. yes b. no
2. What class was Fraser going to miss on Saturday?
   a. acting class b. tap dancing class

After you read

COMPREHENSION

A. Circle the correct answers.

1. On what day did Tom and Fraser have acting lessons?
   a. Monday b. Tuesday c. Saturday
2. Where did they go for their acting lessons?
   a. to the city b. to the school hall c. to their English class
3. When was football training?
   a. before school b. at lunchtime c. after school
4. What did Heath talk about to all the students in the hall?
   a. *Hamlet* b. football c. the play competition

B. Circle T for true or F for false for these sentences.

1. Tom and Fraser both wanted to be actors. T / F
2. Mr Rankin wanted Tom to play football on Saturday. T / F
3. Heath Mason was a teacher at Tom and Fraser's school. T / F
4. Heath said the best actor in the competition would go on TV. T / F

C. Complete these sentences.

1. Fraser was going to see *Hamlet* with his ________.
2. Mr Rankin told Tom to forget about going to the ________.
3. In the hall, Tom and Fraser went up onto the ________.
4. 'There will be prizes for the best play and the best ________.'

D. Write short answers to these questions.

1. Who was the biggest boy in the football team?
____
2. What school was Tom's team playing against on Saturday?
____
3. What was the name of the school principal?
____
4. Where did all the classes have to go that afternoon?
____

LANGUAGE ACTIVITIES

A. Write the correct prepositions in the spaces.

of on from to

1. Tom has to play football ________ Saturday.
2. It's the biggest game ________ the year.
3. Heath talked ________ all the students in the school.
4. There was a lot of noise ________ the students.

B. Write the missing letters to make words from Chapter 1.

1. _ft_rn_ _n
2. c_ _ch
3. tr_ _n_ng
4. c_mp_t_t_ _n

WHAT DO YOU THINK?

Listen to Chapter 1 on the CD. Do you think Tom and Fraser will go in the competition? Will they do well? Why or why not?

____

Chapters 2 and 3

Before you read

A. Look at the picture on page 15 and circle the correct answers.

1. Where are the boys?
   a. in a house b. in a classroom c. in a theatre
2. How do you think their meeting looks?
   a. quiet b. noisy

B. Find these words in your dictionary. Use them in the sentences.

excited library myth rehearse

1. I was __________ because it was the night before Christmas.
2. If you want to do a play you have to __________ a lot.
3. I went to the __________ to borrow a book.
4. The teacher read the class a __________ from ancient Rome.

C. Listen to Track 4 on the CD and answer these questions.

1. How many boys came and spoke with Tom and Fraser?
   a. two b. four
2. How did Tom and Fraser feel when their friends said they wanted to be in the play?
   a. angry b. surprised
3. How did Anton feel about being in a play?
   a. He wanted to be in it. b. He didn't want to be in it.

After you read

Comprehension

A. Circle the correct answers.

1. What kind of play did Luke want the group to do?
   a. a funny play b. a sad play c. a play by Shakespeare
2. Who suggested that the group do *Monkey Man*?
   a. Tom b. Anton c. Luke
3. Why did Tom get called off the football field?
   a. Because he was ill. b. Because he was playing badly.
   c. Because he was fighting with Gary.
4. Who did Tom decide could be Prometheus in the play?
   a. Anton b. Fraser c. Luke

B. Circle T for true or F for false for these sentences.

1. Anton and Luke had never been in a play before. T / F
2. Tom asked his grandmother for some books of plays. T / F
3. Gary was the best player in the game on Saturday. T / F
4. Anton said he wanted to be Prometheus. T / F

C. Complete these sentences.

1. Lots of boys were looking for books of plays in the library.
2. In *Taylor, Taylor,* the boy and the girl had the same name.
3. Tom's grandfather gave him a big old book.
4. In the myth, Prometheus made men out of clay.

D. Write short answers to these questions.

1. What was the name of the play Anton suggested?
   Romeo and Juliet
2. What was the name of the play Tom was writing?
   Fire light
3. In the myth, what did Prometheus give to men?
   fire
4. Who did Tom decide Luke could be in the play?
   Zeus

Language activities

A. Match the words that go together in Chapters 2 and 3.

1. football — pot
2. flower — school
3. coffee — field
4. acting — cup

B. Use these letters to write words from Chapters 2 and 3.

1. ymht myth
2. yalc clay
3. daei idea
4. puogr group

What do you think?

Listen to Chapters 2 and 3 on the CD. Do you think the boys will be able to stop fighting and put on a good play? Why or why not?

Yes. Because the like the price

Chapter 4

Before you read

A. Look at the picture on page 24 and circle the correct answers.

1. What are the boys doing?
   a. watching a play b. writing a play c. rehearsing their play
2. Where are they?
   a. in a classroom b. at Tom's house c. on the football field

B. Find these words in your dictionary. Use them in the sentences.

mask glandular fever changed costume

1. My clothes are dirty. I'll get __________ before dinner.
2. He was wearing a __________ so I couldn't see his face.
3. She had a beautiful __________. It was a long red dress.
4. Jim got __________ and couldn't come to school for five weeks.

C. Listen to Track 5 on the CD and answer these questions.

1. How did Mr Rankin speak to Gary?
   a. kindly b. angrily
2. What did Gary say footballers should do?
   a. only play football b. lots of different things
3. Did Tom agree with what Gary said about the play?
   a. yes b. no

After you read

Comprehension

A. Circle the correct answers.

1. Who made the costumes for the play?
   a. Tom's mother b. Mr Rankin c. Anton and his mother
2. Who got glandular fever?
   a. Fraser b. Anton c. Luke
3. Why couldn't Gary play in the game on Saturday?
   a. Because he hit Tom. b. Because Tom hit him.
   c. Because he was ill.
4. Where did Tom go after the game on Saturday?
   a. to Fraser's house b. to Gary's house c. to Anton's house

B. Circle T for true or F for false for these sentences.

1. Gary said Tom's play was very good. T / F
2. Anton was sick but he could still be in the play. T / F
3. Gary played in the second half of the football game. T / F
4. Mr Howard was friendly towards Tom. T / F

C. Complete these sentences.

1. Anton had to stay home from school for a few weeks.
2. The day of the last football game was cold and wet.
3. Anton said he wanted to see his friends win the competition
4. Tom looked for the bag in the changing room but it was ________.

D. Write short answers to these questions.

1. What colour was Zeus's coat?
   Purple
2. Who brought the masks and costumes to the football field?
   Mrs Mitchel
3. Who took the costumes and masks?
   Gary
4. Who asked Gary to be in the play?
   Tom

Language activities

A. Write the correct prepositions in the spaces.

out up out about

1. Get up off the ground!
2. Think about that!
3. Go out there and win!
4. Get out of my room!

B. Write the missing letters to make words from Chapter 4.

1. h o p e l e ss
2. g o ld e n
3. n a sty
4. st u p e d

What do you think?

Listen to Chapter 4 on the CD. Will the other boys be happy that Tom asked Gary to be in the play?

No not really

Chapter 5

Before you read

A. Look at the picture on page 33 and circle the correct answers.

1. Where are the boys?
   a. at Tom's house   b. in a classroom   c. on stage in the hall
2. How does the man look?
   a. angry   b. happy   c. sad

B. Find these words in your dictionary. Use them in the sentences.

circle   stick   bowl   forgot

1. I had a __________ of soup for dinner.
2. The children all held hands and stood in a __________.
3. I tried to sing the song, but I __________ the words.
4. The old man had to use a __________ to help him to walk.

C. Listen to Track 6 on the CD and answer these questions.

1. How did Fraser and Luke react to Tom's news?
   a. They were shocked.   b. They were happy.
2. How long did they have before the competition?
   a. one week   b. two weeks
3. Did Fraser and Luke agree to try doing the play with Gary?
   a. yes   b. no

After you read

Comprehension

A. Circle the correct answers.

1. What did Gary often forget during rehearsals?
   a. his costume   b. his words   c. his mask
2. Who told the boys to stop the rehearsal of their play?
   a. Mr Barton   b. Mr Rankin   c. Mr Howard
3. Where did the boys take the people to see their play?
   a. to the football field   b. to Anton's house   c. to the hall
4. Which play won the competition?
   a. *Macbeth*   b. *Here and Now*   c. *Fire Light*

B. Circle T for true or F for false for these sentences.

1. One group of boys did a part of *Macbeth* as their play. T / F
2. Anton acted in *Fire Light*. T / F
3. The people liked *Fire Light*. T / F
4. Gary hated being an actor. T / F

C. Complete these sentences.

1. The groups had to rehearse in front of the teachers and the principal.
2. Fraser put the stick that was on fire into a golden bowl.
3. Tom asked the people to stand in a big circle.
4. Tom thanked Heath for bringing plays back to the school.

D. Write short answers to these questions.

1. What kind of play did the second group do?
   funny play
2. What did Mr Barton say the boys couldn't have on the stage?
   fire
3. Who won the prize for the best actor?
   Fraser McDonald
4. Who did Heath want the writer of *Fire Light* to meet?
   ____

Language activities

A. Write the correct prepositions in the spaces.

onto out off in

1. Mr Barton told Tom's group to get __________ the stage.
2. People slowly went __________ of the hall.
3. The stars shone __________ the sky.
4. They went __________ the football field.

B. Write the missing letters to make words from Chapter 4 and 5.

1. r _ h_ _ rs _
2. cl _ p
3. ch _ _ r
4. d _ nc _

What do you think?

Listen to Chapter 5 on the CD. Have you ever acted in a play? Did you enjoy it, or would you like to try it? Why or why not?

____

Glossary

adj. adjective; *n.* noun; *v.* verb

act /ækt/ *v.*	darstellen; aufführen
acting /ˈæktɪŋ/ *n.*	Schauspielerei
actor /ˈæktə/ *n.*	Schauspieler
changing room /ˈtʃeɪndʒɪŋ ˌruːm/ *n.*	Umkleideraum
cheer /tʃɪə/ *v.*	jubeln
clap /klæp/ *v.*	klatschen
clay /kleɪ/ *n.*	Ton, Lehm
coach /kəʊtʃ/ *n.*	Trainer
competition /ˌkɒmpəˈtɪʃn/ *n.*	Wettbewerb
costume /ˈkɒstjuːm/ *n.*	Kostüm
drum /drʌm/ *n.*	Trommel
fight /faɪt/ *v.*	kämpfen; (sich) streiten
n.	Kampf; Streit
get changed /get tʃeɪndʒd/ *v.*	sich umziehen
glandular fever /ˈglændjʊlə fiːvə/ *n.*	Drüsenfieber
gods /gɒdz/ *n.*	Götter
golden /ˈgəʊld(ə)n/ *adj.*	golden/e/r
group /gruːp/ *n.*	Gruppe
hall /hɔːl/ *n.*	Aula; Halle
hopeless /ˈhəʊpləs/ *adj.*	hoffnungslos
idea /aɪˈdɪə/ *n.*	Idee
mask /mɑːsk/ *n.*	Maske
mirror /ˈmɪrə/ *n.*	Spiegel
myth /mɪθ/ *n.*	Mythos
old boy /əʊld bɔɪ/ *n.*	ehemaliger Schüler, Ehemaliger

play /pleɪ/ *n.*	Theaterstück, Drama
v.	Theater spielen; spielen
player /ˈpleɪə/ *n.*	Spieler
principal /ˈprɪnsəpl/ *n.*	Schuldirektor
prize /praɪz/ *n.*	Preis
put on (a play) /pʊt ɒn/ *v.*	aufführen
rehearse /rɪˈhɜːs/ *v.*	proben, einüben
show /ʃəʊ/ *n.*	Aufführung; (Fernseh)Show
v.	zeigen; erklären
stage /steɪdʒ/ *n.*	Bühne
steal /stiːl/ *v.*	stehlen
tap dancing /tæp ˈdɑːnsɪŋ/ *n.*	Stepptanz
training /ˈtreɪnɪŋ/ *n.*	Training
win /wɪn/ *v.*	gewinnen
yell /jel/ *v.*	jubeln, rufen